"Do give books - religious or otherwise - for Christmas.
They're never fattening, seldom sinful, and permanently personal."

Lenore Hershey

The Big Christmas Songbook

EXCLUSIVELY DISTRIBUTED BY

HAL•LEONARD®

Exclusive Distributors:
Music Sales Limited
14/15 Berners Street, London W1T 3LJ,
United Kingdom.

Music Sales Corporation
257 Park Avenue South,
New York, NY 10010,
United States of America.

Music Sales Pty Limited
20 Resolution Drive, Caringbah, NSW 2229,
Australia.

Order No. AM993696
ISBN 978-1-84772-566-0
This book © Copyright 2008 Wise Publications,
a division of Music Sales Limited.

Compiled & edited by Ann Barkway.
Music processed by Barnes Music Engraving.
Illustrated by Arlene Adams.
Front cover 'bow' illustrated by Mark Thomas.
Printed in China.
CD recorded, mixed and mastered by Jonas Persson.
Backing tracks by Rick Cardinali.
Vocals by Rachael Parsons.

Your Guarantee of Quality
As publishers, we strive to produce every
book to the highest commercial standards.
The music has been freshly engraved
and the book has been carefully designed to
minimise awkward page turns and to make
playing from it a real pleasure.
Throughout, the printing and binding have
been planned to ensure a sturdy, attractive
publication which should give years of enjoyment.
If your copy fails to meet our high standards,
please inform us and we will gladly replace it.

www.musicsales.com

Poems...

Stories...

Music...

Away In A Manger

Words **Traditional**   *Music by* **William Kirkpatrick**

Gently

A - way in a___ man - ger, no___ crib for a bed, The___ lit - tle Lord Je - sus laid___

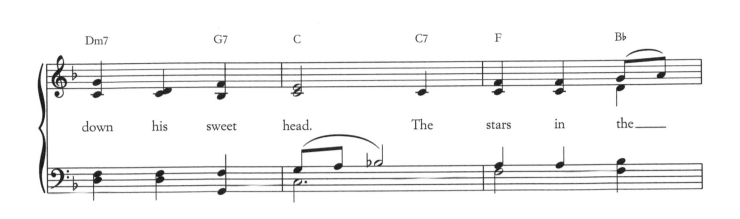

down his sweet head. The stars in the___

bright sky looked_ down where he lay, The___

lit - tle Lord Je - sus a - sleep on the hay.

2 The cattle are lowing, the baby awakes,
But little Lord Jesus no crying he makes.
I love thee, Lord Jesus! Look down from the sky,
And stay by my side until morning is nigh.

3 Be near me, Lord Jesus; I ask thee to stay
Close by me for ever, and love me, I pray.
Bless all the dear children in thy tender care,
And fit us for heaven, to live with thee there.

Away *In A Manger*

American Tune Words **Traditional**   *Music by* **James R. Murray**

Tenderly

A - way in a man - ger, no crib for a

bed, The lit - tle Lord Je - sus laid

down his sweet head. The stars in the

sky_____ looked down where he lay, The

lit - tle Lord Je - sus a - sleep on the hay.

2 The cattle are lowing, the baby awakes,
But little Lord Jesus no crying he makes.
I love thee, Lord Jesus! Look down from the sky,
And stay by my side until morning is nigh.

3 Be near me, Lord Jesus; I ask thee to stay
Close by me for ever, and love me, I pray.
Bless all the dear children in thy tender care,
And fit us for heaven, to live with thee there.

Deck *The* Hall

Traditional

TRACK 3

Brightly

Deck the hall with boughs of hol - ly, Fa la la la la, la

la la la, 'Tis the sea - son to be jol - ly, Fa la la la la, la

The Big Christmas Songbook

8

la la la, Don we now our gay ap - pa - rel,

Fa la la, la la la, la la la, Troll the an - cient

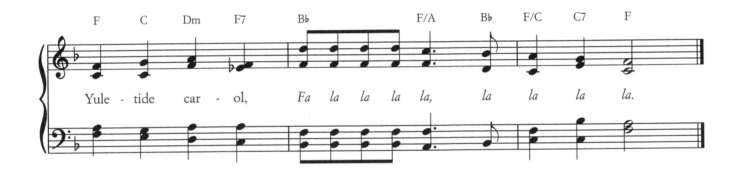

Yule - tide car - ol, Fa la la la la, la la la la.

See the flowing bowl before us,
Fa la la la la la la la la la,
Strike the harp and join the chorus,
Fa la la la la la la la la la,

2 Follow me in merry measure,
Fa la la la la la la la la la,
While I sing of beauty's treasure,
Fa la la la la la la la la la.

Fast away the old year passes,
Fa la la la la la la la la la,
Hail the new, ye lads and lasses,
Fa la la la la la la la la la,

3 Laughing, quaffing, all together,
Fa la la la la la la la la la,
Heedless of the wind and weather.
Fa la la la la la la la la la.

TRACK 4

The *Coventry* Carol

Traditional

Lul - lay, thou lit - tle ti - ny child,

By by, lul - lay, lul - lay; _____ Lul -

- lay,   thou   lit - tle   ti - ny   child,

By   by,   lul - lay,   lul - lay._____

2 O sisters too, how may we do,
For to preserve this day
This poor youngling, for whom we sing
By by, lullay, lullay?

3 Herod the King in his raging,
Chargèd he hath this day
His men of might, in his own sight,
All children young to slay.

4 Then woe is me, poor child, for thee,
And ever, morn and day,
For thy parting nor say nor sing,
By by, lullay, lullay.

Ding Dong Merrily On High

Music **Traditional**   Words by **George Woodward**

Ding dong! mer-ri-ly on high,   in heaven the bells are ring-ing,

Ding dong! ve-ri-ly the sky is riven with an-gels sing - ing.

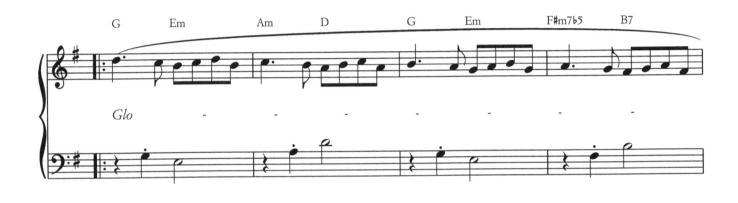

Glo - - - - - - -

- - - - ri - a, Ho - san - na in ex - cel - sis.

Chorus *Gloria, hosanna in excelsis.*

2
E'en so here below, below,
Let steeple bells be swungen,
And i-o, i-o, i-o,
By priest and people sungen.
Gloria, hosanna in excelsis...

3
Pray you, dutifully prime
Your matin chime, ye ringers;
May you beautifully rhyme
Your evetime song, ye singers.
Gloria, hosanna in excelsis...

William's *Home* Coming *At* Christmas *from* Sons & Lovers *by* D.H. Lawrence

They were very poor that autumn. William had just gone away to London, and his mother missed his money. He sent ten shillings once or twice, but he had many things to pay for at first. His letter came regularly once a week. He wrote a good deal to his mother, telling her all his life, how he made friends, and was exchanging lessons with a Frenchman, how he enjoyed London. His mother felt again he was remaining to her just as when he was at home. She wrote to him every week her direct, rather witty letters. All day long, as she cleaned the house, she thought of him. He was in London: he would do well. Almost, he was like her knight who wore *her* favour in the battle.

He was coming at Christmas for five days. There had never been such preparations. Paul and Arthur scoured the land for holly and evergreens. Annie made the pretty paper hoops in the old-fashioned way. And there was unheard-of-extravagance in the larder. Mrs Morel made a big and magnificent cake. Then, feeling queenly, she showed Paul how to blanch almonds. He skinned the long nuts reverently, counting them all, to see not one was lost. It was said that eggs whisked better in a cold place. So the boy stood in the scullery, where the temperature was nearly at freezing point, and whisked and whisked, and flew in excitement to his mother as the white of egg grew stiffer and more snowy.

'Just look, mother! Isn't it lovely?'

And he balanced a bit on his nose, then blew it in the air.

'Now, don't waste it,' said the mother.

Everybody was mad with excitement. William was coming on Christmas Eve. Mrs Morel surveyed the pantry. There was a big plum cake, and a rice cake, jam tarts, lemon tarts, and mince-pies – two enormous dishes. She was finishing

cooking – Spanish tarts and cheesecakes. Everywhere was decorated. The kissing bunch of berried holly hung with bright and glittering things, spun slowly over Mrs Morel's head as she trimmed her little tarts in the kitchen. A great fire roared. There was scent of cooked pastry. He was due at seven o'clock, but he would be late. The three children had gone to meet him. She was alone. But at a quarter to seven Morel came in again. Neither wife nor husband spoke. He sat in his armchair, quite awkward with excitement, and she quietly went on with her baking. Only by the careful way in which she did things could it be told how much moved she was. The clock ticked on.

'What time dost say he's coming?' Morel asked for the fifth time.

'The train gets in at half past six,' she replied emphatically.

'Then he'll be here at ten past seven.'

'Eh, Bless you, it'll be hours late on the Midland,' she said indifferently. But she hoped, by expecting him late, to bring him early. Morel went down the entry to look for him. The he came back.

'Goodness, man!' she said. 'You're like an ill-setting hen.'

'Hadna you better be getting' him summat t'eat ready?' asked the father.

'There's plenty of time,' she answered.

'There's not much *I* can see on,' he answered, turning crossly in his chair. She began to clear the table. The kettle was singing. They waited and waited.

Meantime the three children were on the platform at Sethley Bridge, on the Midland main line, two miles from home. They waited one hour. A train came – he was not there. Down the line the red and green lights shone. It was very dark and very cold.

'Ask him if the London train's come,' said Paul to Annie, when they saw a man in a tip cap.

'I'm not,' said Annie. 'You be quiet – he might send us off.'

But Paul was dying for the man to know they were expecting someone by the London train: it sounded so grand. Yet he was much too much scared of broaching any man, let alone one in a peaked cap, to dare to ask. The three children could scarcely go into the waiting-room for the fear of being sent away, and for fear something should happen whilst they were off the platform. Still they waited in the dark and cold.

'It's an hour an' a half late,' said Arthur pathetically.

'Well' said Annie, 'it's Christmas Eve.'

They all grew silent. He wasn't coming. They looked down the darkness of the

railway. There was London! It seemed the uttermost of distance. They thought anything might happen if one came from London. They were all too troubled to talk. Cold and unhappy, and silent, they huddled together on the platform.

At last, after more than two hours, they saw the lights of an engine peering round, away down the darkness. A porter ran out. The children drew back with beating hearts. A great train bound for Manchester drew up. Two doors opened, and from one of them, William. They flew to him. He handed parcels to them cheerily, and immediately began to explain that this great train had stopped for *his* sake at such a small station as Sethley Bridge: it was not booked to stop.

Meanwhile the parents where getting anxious. The table was set, the chop was cooked, everything was ready. Mrs Morel put her on her black apron. She was wearing her best dress. Then she sat, pretending to read. The minutes were a torture to her.

'H'm!' said Morel. 'It's an hour an' a ha'ef.'

'And those children waiting!' she said.

'Th' train canna ha' come in yet,' he said.

'I tell you, on Christmas Eve they're *hours* wrong.'

They were both a bit cross with each other, so gnawed with anxiety. The ash-tree moaned outside in a cold, raw wind. And all that space of night from London home! Mrs Morel suffered. The slight click of the works inside the clock irritated her. It was getting so late; it was getting unbearable.

At last there was a sound of voices, and a footstep in the entry.

'Ha's here!' cried Morel, jumping up.

Then he stood back The mother ran a few steps towards the door and waited. There was a rush and a patter of feet, the door burst open. William was there. He dropped his Gladstone bag and took his mother in his arms.

'Mater!' he said.

'My boy!' she cried.

And for two seconds, no longer, she clasped him and kissed him. Then she withdrew and said, trying to be quite normal:

'But how late you are!'

'Aren't I!' he cried, turning to his father. 'Well, dad!'

The two men shook hands.

'Well, my lad!'

Morel's eyes were wet.

'We thought tha'd niver be commin',' he said.

'Oh, I'd come!' exclaimed William.

Then the son turned to his mother.

'But you look well,' she said proudly, laughing.

'Well' he exclaimed. 'I should think so – coming home!'

He was a fine fellow, big, straight, and fearless-looking. He looked round at the evergreens and the kissing bunch, and the little tarts that lay in their tins on the hearth.

'By jove! mother, it's not different!' he said, as if in relief.

Everybody was still for a second. Then he suddenly sprang forward, picked a tart from the hearth, and pushed it whole into his mouth.

'Well, did iver you see such a parish oven!' the father exclaimed.

He had brought them endless presents. Every penny he had he had spent on them. There was a sense of luxury overflowing in the house. For his mother there was an umbrella with gold on the pale handle. She kept it to her dying day, and would have lost anything rather than that. Everybody had something gorgeous, and besides, there were pounds of unknown sweets: Turkish delight, crystallised pineapple, and such-like things which, the children thought, only the splendour of London could provide. And Paul boasted of these sweets among his friends.

'Real pineapple, cut off in slices, and then turned into crystal – fair grand!'

Everybody was mad with happiness in the family. Home was home, and they loved it with a passion of love, whatever the suffering had been. There were parties, there were rejoicings. People came in to see William, to see what difference London had made to him. And they all found him 'such a gentlemen, and *such* a fine fellow, my word!'

Long, Long Ago
Anon

Winds through the olive trees
    Softly did blow
Round little Bethlehem
    Long, long ago.

Sheep on the hillside lay
    Whiter than snow
Shepherds were watching them
    Long, long ago.

Then from the happy sky,
    Angels bent low
Singing their songs of joy,
    Long, long ago.

For in a manger bed,
    Cradled we know
Christ came to Bethlehem
    Long, long ago.

Hark! *The* Herald *Angels* Sing

Music by **Felix Mendelssohn**   Words by *Charles Wesley*

Hark! The her-ald an-gels sing___ Glo-ry to the new-born king;

Peace on earth, and mer-cy mild,___ God and sin-ners re-con-ciled.

Joy - ful, all you na - tions, rise, ___ Join the tri - umph of the skies; ___

With th'an - gel - ic hosts pro - claim, Christ is ___ born in Beth - le - hem.

Hark! The her - ald an - gels sing, Glo - ry ___ to the new - born King.

Chorus *Hark! The herald angels sing,*
Glory to the newborn King.

2	Christ, by highest heav'n adored,	3	Hail, the heav'n-born Prince of Peace!
	Christ, the everlasting Lord,		Hail, the Sun of Righteousness!
	Late in time behold him come,		Light and life to all he brings,
	Offspring of a Virgin's womb!		Ris'n with healing in his wings;
	Veiled in flesh the Godhead see,		Mild he lays His glory by,
	Hail, the incarnate Deity!		Born that we no more may die,
	Pleased as man with man to dwell,		Born to raise us from the earth,
	Jesus, our Emmanuel.		Born to give us second birth.
	Hark! The herald angels sing etc...		*Hark! The herald angels sing etc...*

TRACK 7

I *Saw* Three *Ships*

Traditional

I saw three ships come sail-ing in, On Christ-mas Day, on Christ-mas Day; I

saw three ships come sail-ing in, On Christ-mas Day in the morn-ing.

2 And what was in those ships all three?
On Christmas Day, on Christmas Day,
And what was in those ships all three?
On Christmas Day in the morning.

3 Our Saviour Christ and his lady.
On Christmas Day, on Christmas Day,
Our Saviour Christ and his lady.
On Christmas Day in the morning.

4 Pray, whither sailed those ships all three?
On Christmas Day, on Christmas Day,
Pray, whither sailed those ships all three?
On Christmas Day in the morning.

5 O, they sailed into Bethlehem.
On Christmas Day, on Christmas Day,
O, they sailed into Bethlehem.
On Christmas Day in the morning.

6 And all the bells on earth shall ring.
On Christmas Day, on Christmas Day,
And all the bells on earth shall ring.
On Christmas Day in the morning.

7 And all the angels in heaven shall sing.
On Christmas Day, on Christmas Day,
And all the angels in heaven shall sing.
On Christmas Day in the morning.

8 And all the souls on earth shall sing.
On Christmas Day, on Christmas Day,
And all the souls on earth shall sing.
On Christmas Day in the morning.

9 Then let us all rejoice amain!
On Christmas Day, on Christmas Day,
Then let us all rejoice amain!
On Christmas Day in the morning.

In *Dulci* Jubilo

Traditional   *English Words by* **R.L. Pearsall**

Moderately

In dul - ci ju - bi - lo_____ Let us our hom - age show;_____ Our heart's joy re - cli - neth In prae - se - pi - o,_____ And like a bright star

shi - neth Ma - tris in gre - mi -

-o; Al - pha es et O,

Al - pha es et O!

O Jesu parvule!
My heart is sore for thee!
Hear me, I beseech thee,
O puer optime!
My prayer let it reach thee
O Princeps gloriae!
Trahe me post te!
Trahe me post te!

2

O Patris caritas!
O nati lenitas!
Deep were we stainèd
Per nostra crimina;
But thou has for us gainèd
Coelorum gaudia:
O that we were there,
O that we were there!

3

Ubi sunt gaudia, where,
If that they be not there?
There, are angels singing
Nova cantica;
There the bells are ringing
In Regis curia:
O that we were there,
O that we were there!

4

Infant *Holy*, Infant *Lowly*

Traditional Polish

Moderately

G   D/F♯   G/B   Am/C   D⁷

In - fant ho - ly, in - fant low - ly, For His bed a cat - tle

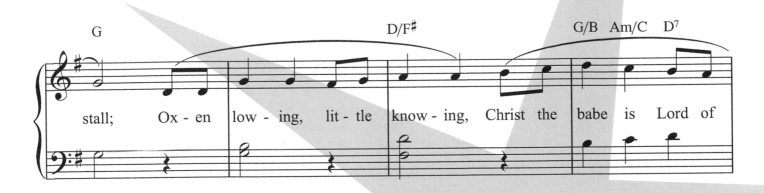

stall; Ox - en low - ing, lit - tle know - ing, Christ the babe is Lord of

all. Swift are wing - ing an - gels sing - ing, Now - ells ring - ing, tid - ings

bring - ing, Christ the babe is Lord of all, Christ the babe is Lord of all.

2 Flocks were sleeping, shepherds keeping
Vigil 'til the morning new,
Saw the glory, heard the story,
Tidings of a gospel true.
Thus rejoicing, free from sorrow,
Praises voicing, greet the morrow,
Christ the babe was born for you,
Christ the babe was born for you.

Jingle *Bells*

Words & Music by **J. S. Pierpont**

Moderately, with bounce

Jin - gle bells, jin - gle bells, jin - gle all the

way, Oh, what fun it is to ride in a

one - horse o - pen sleigh. one - horse o - pen sleigh.

Chorus

Jingle bells, jingle bells,
Jingle all the way,
Oh, what fun it is to ride
In a one-horse open sleigh.

2   A day or two ago
I thought I'd take a ride,
And soon Miss Fannie Bright
Was seated by my side;
The horse is lean and lank,
Misfortune seemed his lot,
He got into a drifted bank,
And then we got upsot!
Jingle bells, jingle bells...

The *Snow*-man
by Mabel *Marlowe*

A snow-man once stood upon a hill, with his face towards the sunset. A very fine snow-man he was, as tall as a soldier, and much fatter. He had two pieces of glass for eyes, and a stone for a nose, and a piece of black wood for a mouth, and in his hand he held a stout, knobbly club. But he had no clothes at all, not even a hat, and the wind on the top of that hill was as bitter as wind could be.

"How cold I am! I am as cold as ice," said the snow-man. "But that red sky looks warm."

So he lifted his feet from the ground, and went tramp, tramp, tramping down the slope towards the setting sun.

Very soon he overtook a gipsy woman, who was wearing a bright red shawl.

"Ha, that looks warm! I must have it," thought the snow-man.

So he went up to the gipsy woman and he said, "Give me that red shawl."

"No, indeed! I cannot spare it on this wintry day," answered the gipsy. "I am cold enough as it is."

"Cold?" shouted the snow-man in a very growlish voice. "Are you as cold as I am, I wonder? Are you cold inside as well as outside? Are you made of ice, through and through and through?"

"No, I suppose not," mumbled the gipsy, who was getting hot with fright.

"Then give me your red shawl this moment, or I shall strike you with my stout, knobbly club."

Then the gipsy took off her red shawl, grumbling all the time, and gave it to the snow-man. He put it round his shoulders, without a word of thanks, and went tramp, tramp, tramping down the hill. And the shivering gipsy followed behind him.

Presently, the snow-man overtook a ploughboy who was wearing his grand-mother's long, red woollen mittens.

"Ha, they look warm! I must have them," thought the snow-man.

So he went up to the ploughboy and he said, "Give me those red woollen mittens."

"No, indeed!" said the ploughboy. "They belong to my grandmother. She lent them to me because my fingers were so cold."

"Cold?" shouted the snow-man, in a very roarish voice. "Are your fingers as cold as mine, I wonder? Are your hands and arms frozen into ice, through and through and through?"

"No, I suppose not," mumbled the ploughboy.

"Then give me those red mittens, this moment, or I shall strike you with my stout, knobbly club."

So the ploughboy drew off the warm mittens, grumbling all the time, and the snow-man put them on, without a word of thanks. Then he went tramp, tramp, tramping down the hill. And the gipsy and the ploughboy followed him.

After a while he overtook a tame pirate, wearing a pirate's thick red cap, with a tassel dangling down his back.

"Ha! That looks warm! I must have it," said the snow-man.

So he went up to the tame pirate and he said, "Give me that red tassel cap."

"No, indeed!" said the pirate. "A nice cold in the head I should get if I did."

"Cold in the head?" shouted the snow-man, in a very thunderish voice. "Is your head as cold as mine, I wonder? Are your brains made of snow, and your bones solid ice, through and through and through?"

"No, I suppose not," muttered the tame pirate.

"Then give me that red tassel cap, this moment, or I shall set upon you with my stout, knobbly club."

Now the pirate felt very sorry that he had turned tame, but he did not like the look of that knobbly stick, so he gave up his red tassel cap. The snow-man put it on without a word of thanks. Then he went tramp, tramp, tramping down the hill, with the tassel bumping up and down. And the gipsy woman, and the ploughboy, and the tame pirate followed him.

At last he reached the bottom of the hill, where the village school house stood, and there was the village schoolmaster on the doorstep, looking at the sunset. He was smoking a glowing briar pipe, and on his feet were two red velvet slippers.

"Ha! Those look warm! I must have them," said the snow-man.

So he went up to the schoolmaster and said, "Give me those red slippers."

"Certainly, if you want them," said the schoolmaster. "Take them by all means. It is far too cold today to be tramping about with bare toes," and he stooped and drew off his slippers, and there he stood in some bright red socks, thick and woolly and knitted by hand.

"Ha! Those look warm! Give them to me!" said the snow-man.

"Certainly, if you want them," said the schoolmaster. "But you must come inside. I cannot take my socks off here, in the doorway. Come on to the mat."

So the snow-man stepped inside the doorway, and stood upon the mat.

"Be sharp with those socks. My feet are as cold as solid ice," he grumbled.

"I am sorry to hear that" said the schoolmaster. "But I have a warm red blanket airing over the stove. Come in, sir. Sit on that chair by the fire, sir. Put your cold feet upon this snug red footstool, and let me wrap this red blanket around your legs."

So the snow-man came into the schoolhouse, and sat upon a chair by the glowing fire, and put his feet upon the red footstool, and the schoolmaster wrapped the red blanket round and round and round his legs. (And all this while the gipsy woman, and the ploughboy and the tame pirate were peering in at the window.)

"Are you feeling warmer?" asked the schoolmaster.

"No. I am as cold as an iceberg."

"Come closer to the fire."

So the schoolmaster pushed the chair closer to the fire, but the snow-man gave him not one word of thanks.

"Are you feeling warmer now?"

"No. I am as cold as a stone. My feet feel like icy water."

"Move closer to the fire," said the schoolmaster, and he pushed the chair right against the kerb. "There! Are you warmer now?"

"No, no, no! I am colder than ever. I cannot feel my feet at all; I cannot feel my legs at all; I cannot feel my back at all."

Then the schoolmaster pushed the chair quite close up against the stove.

"Are you warmer now?" he said.

But there was no answer, except a slithery sliding sound, and the drip, drip, drip of black snow-water.

"Dear me!" whispered the snow-man, in a gurgling kind of voice. "I have dropped my stout, knobbly club. My red slippers are floating into the ash-pan. My mittens

are swimming in a little river on the floor. My shawl is gone. My red tassel cap is slipping, slipping away. My head is going... going..."

Splosh! Splash! Gurgle!

"That's the end of him," said the schoolmaster, and he went to fetch the mop.

Then the gipsy woman, and the ploughboy and the tame pirate came in and picked up their things, and wrung them out, and dried them at the stove, and the schoolmaster put his red slippers on the hearth, and hung the red blanket over the back of the chair.

Then he picked up the stout, knobbly club and gave the fire a poke.

Hang Up The Baby's Stocking
Anon

Hang up the baby's stocking! Be sure you don't forget!
The dear little dimpled darling, she never saw Christmas yet!
But I've told her all about it, and she opened her big blue eyes;
And I'm sure she understood it – she looked so funny and wise.

Dear, what a tiny stocking! It doesn't take much to hold
Such little pink toes as baby's away from the frost and cold.
But then, for the baby's Christmas, it will never do at all.
Why! Santa wouldn't be looking for anything half so small.

I know what will do for the baby; I've thought of the very best plan.
I'll borrow a stocking of Grandma's; the longest that ever I can.
And you'll hang it by mine, dear mother, right here in the corner, so!
And leave a letter to Santa, and fasten it on to the toe.

Write – this is the baby's stocking that hangs in the corner here.
You never have seen her, Santa, for she only came this year.
But she's just the blessed'st baby. And now before you go,
Just cram her stocking with goodies, from the top clean down to the toe!

Joy To The World

Words by **Isaac Watts**   Music by **George Frideric Handel**

TRACK 11

Brightly

Joy to the world! The Lord is come; let earth re-

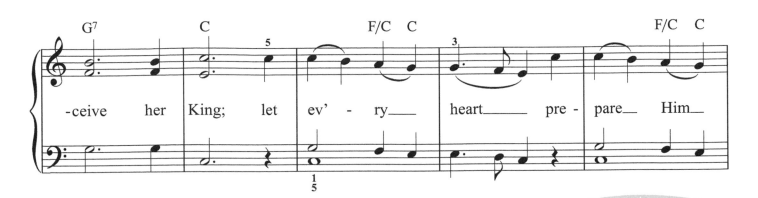

-ceive her King; let ev' - ry___ heart___ pre - pare___ Him___

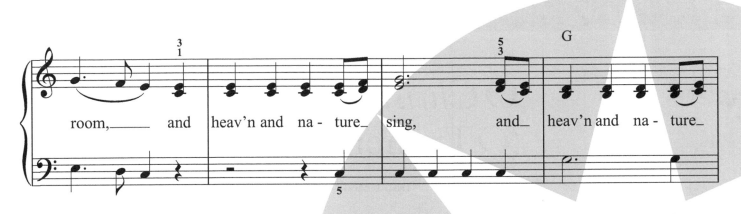

room,___ and heav'n and na - ture___ sing, and___ heav'n and na - ture___

sing, and___ hea - ven, and hea - ven and na - ture sing.

2 Joy to the earth! The Saviour reigns;
Let us our songs employ;
While fields and floods, rocks, hills and plains
Repeat the sounding joy,
Repeat the sounding joy,
Repeat, repeat the sounding joy.

3 He rules the world with truth and grace,
And makes the nations prove
The glories of his righteousness,
And wonders of his love,
And wonders of his love,
And wonders, and wonders of his love.

O *Christmas* Tree (O Tannenbaum)

Traditional

O Christ - mas tree, O Christ - mas tree! Thou tree most fair and

love - ly! O Christ - mas tree, O Christ - mas tree! Thou

Gm Dm Gm7 C7 Fsus4 F F Am7♭5 D7

tree most fair and love - ly! The sight of thee at

Gm C7 Gm7 C7 Fsus F

Christ - mas - tide Spreads hope and glad - ness far and wide, O

F A7♭5 D7sus D7 F Gm Dm Gm7 C7 Fsus F

Christ - mas tree, O Christ - mas tree! Thou tree most fair and love - ly!

2
O Christmas Tree, O Christmas Tree!
Thou hast a wonderous message.
O Christmas Tree, O Christmas Tree!
Thou hast a wonderous message.
Thou dost proclaim the Saviour's birth,
Goodwill to men and peace on earth.
O Christmas Tree, O Christmas Tree!
Thou hast a wonderous message.

O Come, O Come, Emmanuel

Traditional   *English Words by* **John Neale**

The Big Christmas Songbook

36

O come, O come, Em - ma - nu - el, And
ran - som cap - tive Is - ra - el, That
mourns in lone - ly ex - ile here Un -

-til the Son of God_____ ap - pear. Re -

-joice! Re - joice! Em - ma - nu - el shall

come to thee, O Is - - ra - el.

Chorus   *Rejoice! Rejoice!*
Emmanuel shall come to thee, O Israel.

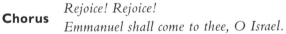

2 O come, thou rod of Jesse, free
Thine own from Satan's tyranny;
From depths of hell thy people save,
And give them vict'ry o'er the grave.
Rejoice! Rejoice!...

3 O come, thou dayspring, come and cheer
Our spirits by thine advent here;
Disperse the gloomy clouds of night,
And death's dark shadows put to flight.
Rejoice! Rejoice!...

4 O come, thou key of David, come,
And open wide our heav'nly home;
Make safe the way that leads on high,
And close the path to misery.
Rejoice! Rejoice!...

5 O come, o come, thou Lord of might,
Who to thy tribes, on Sinai's height
In ancient times didst give the Law
In cloud, and majesty and awe.
Rejoice! Rejoice!...

O Come All Ye Faithful

Original Words & Music by **John Francis Wade**

English Words by **Frederick Oakeley**

TRACK 14

At a moderate pace

O come, all ye faith-ful, Joy-ful and tri-um-phant, O come ye, O come ye to Beth - le - hem.

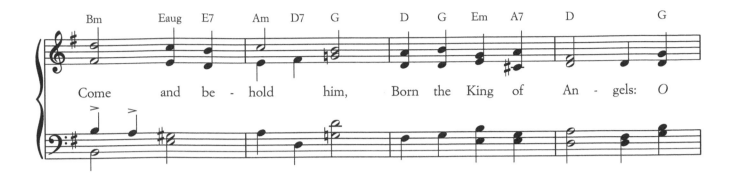

Come and be-hold him, Born the King of An - gels: O

come, let us a - dore him, O come, let us a - dore him, O

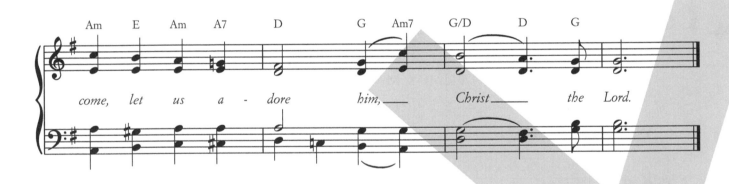

come, let us a - dore him,___ Christ___ the Lord.

Chorus

O come, let us adore him,
O come, let us adore him,
O come, let us adore him,
Christ the Lord.

2
God of God,
Light of light,
Lo! He abhors not the Virgin's womb;
Very God, begotten, not created:
O come, let us adore him…

3
Sing choirs of angels,
Sing in exultation,
Sing all ye citizens of heav'n above;
Glory to God in the highest:
O come, let us adore him…

4
Yea, Lord, we greet thee,
Born this happy morning,
Jesu, to thee be glory giv'n;
Word of the Father, now in flesh appearing:
O come, let us adore him…

O Holy Night

Words & Music by **A. Adam**

With movement

O ho-ly night,___ the stars are bright-ly shin - ing, it is the

night of the dear Sa-viour's birth!___ Long lay the

world___ in sin and er - ror pin - ing, 'til he ap - peared and the

soul felt his worth.___ ___ A thrill of hope the

wea - ry soul re - joi - ces, for yon - der breaks the new and glo - rious

morn! Fall___ ___ on your knees,___ ___ O

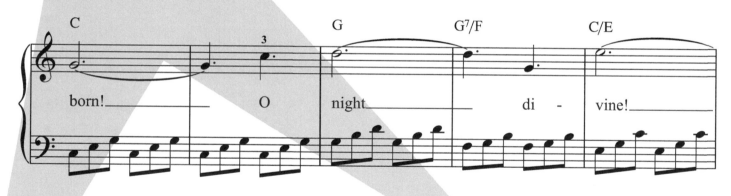

Mr *Pickwick* On *The* Ice
by Charles *Dickens*

Mr Weller and the fat boy, having by their joint endeavours cut out a slide, were exercising themselves thereupon in a very masterly and brilliant manner. Sam Weller, in particular, was displaying that beautiful feat of fancy sliding which is currently denominated 'knocking at the cobbler's door', and which is achieved by skimming over the ice on one foot, and occasionally giving a two-penny postman's knock upon it with the other. It was a good long slide, and there was something in the motion which Mr Pickwick, who was very cold with standing still, could not help envying.

"It looks nice, warm exercise that, doesn't it?" he inquired of Wardle.

"Ah, it does indeed," replied Wardle. "Do you slide?"

"I used to do so, on the gutters, when I was a boy," replied Mr Pickwick.

"Try it now," said Wardle.

"Oh, do, please, Mr Pickwick!" cried all the ladies.

"I should be very happy to afford you any amusement," replied Mr Pickwick, "but I haven't done such a thing these thirty years."

"Pooh! Pooh! Nonsense!" said Wardle. "Here, I'll keep you company. Come along!"

And away went the good-tempered old fellow down the slide, with a rapidity which came very close upon Mr Weller, and beat the fat boy all to nothing.

Mr Pickwick paused, considered, pulled off his gloves and put them in his hat; took two or three short runs, balked himself as often, and at last took another run, and went slowly and gravely down the slide, with his feet about a yard and a quarter apart, amidst the gratified shouts of all the spectators.

"Keep the pot a-bilin', sir!" said Sam; and down went Wardle again, and then Mr Pickwick, and then Sam, and then Mr Winkle, and then Mr Bob Sawyer, and then the fat boy, and then Mr Snodgrass, following closely upon each other's heels, and running after each other with as much eagerness as if all their future prospects in life depended on their expedition.

It was the most intensely interesting thing to observe the manner in which Mr Pickwick performed his share in the ceremony; to watch the torture of anxiety with which he viewed the person behind, gaining upon him at the imminent hazard of tripping him up; to see him gradually expend the painful force which he had put on at first, and turn slowly round on the slide, with his face towards the point from which he had started; to contemplate the playful smile which mantled on his face when he had accomplished the distance, and the eagerness with which he turned round when he had done so and ran after his predecessor – his black gaiters tripping pleasantly through the snow, and his eyes beaming cheerfulness and gladness through his spectacles. And when he was knocked down (which happened upon the average every third round), it was the most invigorating sight that can possibly be imagined to behold him gather up his hat, gloves, and handkerchief, with a glowing countenance, and resume his station in the rank with an ardour and enthusiasm that nothing could abate.

The sport was at its height, the sliding was at the quickest, the laughter was at the loudest, when a sharp, smart crack was heard. There was a quick rush towards the bank, a wild scream from the ladies, and a shout from Mr Tupman.

A large mass of ice disappeared; the water bubbled up over it; Mr Pickwick's hat, gloves, and handkerchief were floating on the surface; and this was all of Mr Pickwick that anybody could see.

Dismay and anguish were depicted on every countenance; the males turned pale, and the females fainted; Mr Snodgrass and Mr Winkle grasped each other by the hand, and gazed at the spot where their leader had gone down, with frenzied eagerness; while Mr Tupman, by way of rendering the promptest assistance, and at the same time conveying to any persons who might be within hearing the clearest possible notion of the catastrophe, ran off across the country at his utmost speed, screaming "Fire!" with all his might.

It was at this very moment, when old Wardle and Sam Weller were approaching the hole with cautious steps, and Mr Benjamin Allen was holding a hurried consultation with Mr Bob Sawyer on the advisability of bleeding the company generally, as an improving little bit of professional practice – it was at this very moment that a face, head, and shoulders emerged from beneath the water, and disclosed the features and spectacles of Mr Pickwick.

"Keep yourself up for an instant – for only one instant!" bawled Mr Snodgrass.

"Yes, do; let me implore you – for my sake!" roared Mr Winkle, deeply affected.

The adjuration was rather unnecessary – the probability being that if Mr Pickwick had declined to keep himself up for anybody else's sake, it would have occurred to him that he might as well do so for his own.

"Do you feel the bottom there, old fellow?" said Wardle.

"Yes, certainly," replied Mr Pickwick, wringing the water from his head and face, and gasping for breath. "I fell upon my back. I couldn't get on my feet at first."

The clay upon so much of Mr Pickwick's coat as was yet visible bore testimony to the accuracy of this statement; and as the fears of the spectators were still further relieved by the fat boy's suddenly recollecting that the water was nowhere more than five feet deep, prodigies of valour were performed to get him out. After a vast quantity of splashing, and cracking, and struggling, Mr Pickwick was at length fairly extricated from his unpleasant position, and once more stood on dry land.

"Oh, he'll catch his death of cold," said Emily.

"Dear old thing!" said Arabella. "Let me wrap this shawl round you, Mr Pickwick."

"Ah, that's the best thing you can do," said Wardle, "and when you've got it on, run home as fast as your legs can carry you, and jump into bed directly."

A dozen shawls were offered on the instant. Three or four of the thickest having been selected, Mr Pickwick was wrapped up, and started off, under the guidance of Mr Weller – presenting the singular phenomenon of an elderly gentleman, dripping wet, and without a hat, with his arms bound down to his sides, skimming over the ground, without any clearly-defined purpose, at the rate of six good English miles an hour.

But Mr Pickwick cared not for appearances in such an extreme case, and urged on by Sam Weller, he kept at the very top of his speed until he reached the door of Manor Farm, where Mr Tupman had arrived some five minutes before, and had frightened the old lady into palpitations of the heart by impressing her with the unalterable conviction that the kitchen chimney was on fire – a calamity which always presented itself in glowing colours to the old lady's mind when anybody about her evinced the smallest agitation.

Mr Pickwick paused not an instant until he was snug in bed.

O Little *Town* Of *Bethlehem*

Words by **Phillips Brooks**   *Music* **Traditional**

At a moderate pace

O lit-tle town of Beth-le-hem, how still we__ see thee lie! A-bove thy deep and dream-less__ sleep the si-lent__ stars go

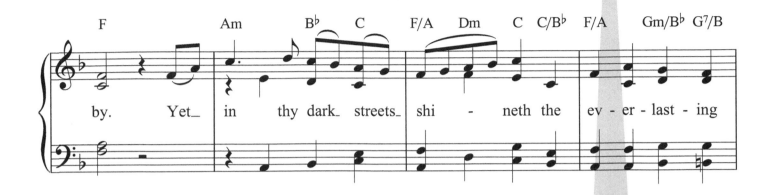

by. Yet_ in thy dark_ streets_ shi - neth the ev - er - last - ing

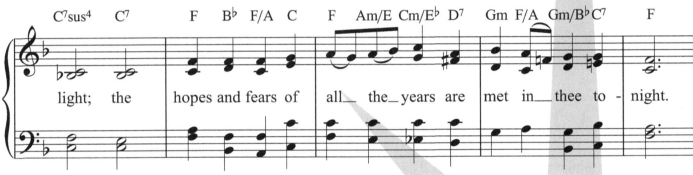

light; the hopes and fears of all_ the_years are met in_thee to - night.

2
O morning stars, together
Proclaim the holy birth,
And praises sing to God the King,
And peace to men on earth!
For Christ is born of Mary;
And, gathered all above,
While mortals sleep, the angels keep
Their watch of wond'ring love.

3
How silently, how silently,
The wond'rous gift is giv'n!
So God imparts to human hearts
The blessings of his heav'n.
No ear may hear his coming;
But in this world of sin,
Where meek souls will receive him, still
The dear Christ enters in.

4
O holy child of Bethlehem,
Descend to us, we pray;
Cast out our sin, and enter in,
Be born in us today.
We hear the Christmas angels
The great glad tidings tell:
O come to us, abide with us,
Our Lord Emmanuel.

O Little *Town* Of Bethlehem

American Tune   Words by **Phillips Brooks**   *Music by* **Lewis H. Redner**

48

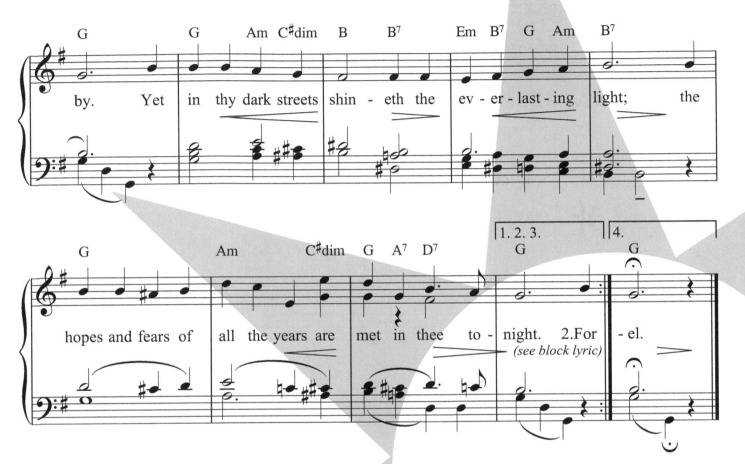

by. Yet in thy dark streets shin - eth the ev - er - last - ing light; the

hopes and fears of all the years are met in thee to - night. 2.For - el.
(see block lyric)

2

O morning stars, together
Proclaim the holy birth,
And praises sing to God the King,
And peace to men on earth!
For Christ is born of Mary;
And, gathered all above,
While mortals sleep, the angels keep
Their watch of wond'ring love.

3

How silently, how silently,
The wondrous gift is giv'n!
So God imparts to human hearts
The blessings of his heav'n.
No ear may hear his coming;
But in this world of sin,
Where meek souls will receive him, still
The dear Christ enters in.

4

O holy child of Bethlehem,
Descend to us, we pray;
Cast out our sin, and enter in,
Be born in us today.
We hear the Christmas angels
The great glad tidings tell:
O come to us, abide with us,
Our Lord Emmanuel.

Past *Three* O'Clock

Words **Traditional**   Music by **George Woodward**

Past three o' clock, And a cold frosty morning,

Past three o' clock; Good morrow, masters all!

Born is a Baby, Gentle as may be,

Son__ of__ the e-ter - nal Fa - ther su - per - nal.

Past three o' clock, And a cold__ fros - ty morn - ing,

Past three o' clock; Good mor - row, mas - ters all!

Chorus

Past three o'clock
And a cold frosty morning,
Past three o'clock;
Good morrow masters all!

2
Seraph quire singeth,
Angel bell ringeth;
Hark how they rime it,
Time it and chime it.
Past three o'clock…

3
Mid earth rejoices
Hearing such voices
Ne'ertofore se well
Carolling Nowell.
Past three o'clock…

4
Light out of star-land
Leadeth from far land
Princes, to meet him,
Worship and greet him.
Past three o'clock…

5
Myrrh from full coffer,
Incense they offer;
Nor is the golden
Nugget witholden.
Past three o'clock…

6
Thus they: I pray you,
Up, sirs, nor stay you
Till ye confess him
Likewise, and bless him.
Past three o'clock…

The *Cratchits* Celebrate Christmas *from* A *Christmas* Carol *by* Charles *Dickens*

Then up rose Mrs Cratchit, Cratchit's wife, dressed out but poorly in a twice-turned gown, but brave in ribbons, which are cheap and make a goodly show for sixpence; and she laid the cloth, assisted by Belinda Cratchit, second of her daughters, also brave in ribbons; while Master Peter Cratchit plunged a fork into the saucepan of potatoes, and getting the corners of his monstrous shirt collar (Bob's private property, confered upon his son and heir in honour of the day) into his mouth, rejoiced to find himself so gallantly attired, and yearned to show his linen in the fashionable Parks. And now two smaller Cratchits, boy and girl, came tearing in, screaming that outside the baker's they had smelt the goose, and known it for their own; and basking in luxurious thoughts of sage and onion, these young Cratchits danced about the table, and exalted Master Peter Cratchit to the skies, while he (not proud, although his collars nearly choked him) blew the fire, until the slow potatoes bubbling up, knocked loudly at the saucepan lid to be let out and peeled.

'What has ever got your precious father then?' said Mrs Cratchit. 'And your brother, Tiny Tim! And Martha warn't as late last Christmas Day by half-an-hour!' 'Here's Martha, Mother!' said a girl, appearing as she spoke.

'Here's Martha, Mother!' cried the two young Cratchits. 'Hurrah! There's *such* a goose, Martha!'

'Why, bless your heart alive, my dear, how late you are!' said Mrs Cratchit, kissing her a dozen times, and taking off her shawl and bonnet for her with officious zeal.

'We'd a deal of work to finish up last night,' replied the girl, 'and had to clear away this morning, Mother!'

'Well! Never mind so long as you are come,' said Mrs Cratchit. 'Sit ye down before the fire, my dear, and have a warm, Lord bless ye!'

No, no! There's Father coming!' cried the two young Cratchits, who were everywhere at once. 'Hide, Martha, hide!'

So Martha hid herself, and in came little Bob, the father, with at least three feet of comforter exclusive of the fringe, hanging down before him; and his threadbare clothes darned up and brushed, to look seasonable; and Tiny Tim upon his shoulder. Alas for Tiny Tim, he bore a little crutch, and had his limbs supported by an iron frame!

'Why, where's our Martha?', cried Bob Cratchit, looking around.

'Not coming,' said Mrs Cratchit.

'Not coming!' said Bob, with a sudden declension in his high spirits; for he had been Tim's blood horse all the way from church, and had come home rampant. 'Not coming upon Christmas Day!'

Martha didn't like to see him disappointed, if it were only in joke; so she came out prematurely from behind the closet door, and ran into his arms, while the two young Cratchits hustled Tiny Tim, and bore him off into the wash-house, that he might hear the pudding singing in the copper.

'And how did little Tim behave?' asked Mrs Cratchit, when she rallied Bob on his credulity, and Bob had hugged his daughter to his heart's content.

'As good as gold,' said Bob, 'and better. Somehow he gets thoughtful, sitting by himself so much, and thinks the strangest things you ever heard. He told me, coming home, that he hoped the people saw him in the church, because he was a cripple, and it might be pleasant to them to remember upon Christmas Day, who made lame beggars walk and blind men see.'

Bob's voice was tremulous when he told them this, and trembled more when he said that Tiny Tim was growing strong and hearty.

His active little crutch was heard upon the floor, and back came Tiny Tim before another word was spoken, escorted by his brother and sister to his stool before the fire; and while Bob, turning up his cuffs - as if, poor fellow, they were capable of being made more shabby - compounded some hot mixture in a jug with gin and lemons, and stirred it round and round and put it on the hob to simmer, Master Peter and the two ubiquitous young Cratchits went to fetch the goose, with which the soon returned in high procession.

Such a bustle ensued that you might have thought a goose the rarest of all birds; a feathered phenomenon, to which a black swan was a matter of course, and in truth it was something very like it in that house. Mrs Cratchit made the gravy

(ready beforehand in a little saucepan) hissing hot; Master Peter mashed the potatoes with incredible vigour; Miss Belinda sweetened up the apple sauce; Martha dusted the hot plates; Bob took Tiny Tim beside him in a tiny corner at the table; the two young Cratchits set chairs for everybody, not forgetting themselves, and mounting guard upon their posts, crammed spoons into their mouths, lest they should shriek for goose before their turn came to be helped. At last the dishes were set on, and grace was said. It was succeeded by a breathless pause, as Mrs Cratchit, looking slowly all along the carving-knife, prepared to plunge it in the breast; but when she did, and when the long-expected gush of stuffing issued forth, one murmur of delight arose all round the   board, and even Tiny Tim, excited by the two young Cratchits, beat on the table with the handle of his knife, and feebly cried Hurrah!

There never was such a goose. Bob said he didn't believe there ever was such a goose cooked. Its tenderness and flavour, size and cheapness, were the themes of universal admiration. Eked out by the apple sauce and mashed potatoes, it was a sufficient dinner for the whole family; indeed, as Mrs Cratchit said with great delight (surveying one small atom of a bone upon the dish), they hadn't ate it all at last! Yet everyone had had enough, and the youngest Cratchits, in particular, were steeped in sage and onion to the eyebrows! But now, the plates being changed by Miss Belinda, Mrs Cratchit left the room alone - too nervous to bear witness - to take the pudding up and bring it in.

Suppose it should not be done enough! Suppose it should break in turning out! Suppose somebody should have got over the wall of the back-yard, and stolen it, while they were merry with the goose - a supposition at which the two young Cratchits became livid! All sorts of horrors were supposed.

Halloa! A great deal of steam! The pudding was out of the copper. A smell like a washing-day! That was the cloth. A smell like an eating-house and a pastry-cook's next door to each other, with a laundress's next door to that! That was the pudding! In half a minute Mrs Cratchit entered - flushed, but smiling proudly - with the pudding, like a speckled cannonball, so hard and firm, blazing in half of half a quartern of ignited brandy, and bedight with Christmas holly stuck into the top.

Oh, a wonderful pudding! Bob Cratchit said, and calmly too, that he regarded it as the greatest success achieved by Mrs Cratchit since their marriage. Mrs Cratchit said that now the weight was off her mind, she would confess she had had her doubts about the quantity of flour. Everybody had something to say about it, but nobody said

or thought it was at all a small pudding for a large family. It would have been flat heresy to do so. Any Cratchit would have blushed to hint at such a thing.

At last the dinner was all done, the cloth was cleared, the hearth swept, and the fire made up. The compound in the jug being tasted, and considered perfect, apples and oranges were put upon the table, and a shovelful of chestnuts upon the fire. Then all the Cratchit family drew round the hearth in what Bob Cratchit called a circle, meaning half a one; and at Bob Cratchit's elbow stood the family display of glass. Two tumblers, and a custard-cup without a handle.

These held the hot stuff from the jug, however, as well as golden goblets would have done; and Bob served it out with beaming looks, while the chestnuts on the fire sputtered and cracked noisily. Then Bob proposed:

'A Merry Christmas to us all, my dears. God bless us!'

Which all the family re-echoed.

'God bless us everyone!' said Tiny Tim, the last of all.

Winter
Lord Tennyson (1809-92)

The frost is here,
The fuel is dear
And woods are sear,
And fires burn clear,
And frost is here
And has bitten the heel of the going year.

Bite, frost, bite!
You roll up away from the light,
The blue-wood-louse and the plump dormouse,
And the bees are stilled and the fires are killed,
And you bite far into the heart of the house,
But not into mine.

Bite, frost, bite!
The woods are all the searer,
The fuel is all the dearer,
The fires are all the clearer,
My spring is all the nearer,
You have bitten into the heart of the earth,
But not into mine

Once *In* Royal *David's* City

Words by **Cecil Alexander**   Music by **Henry Gauntlett**

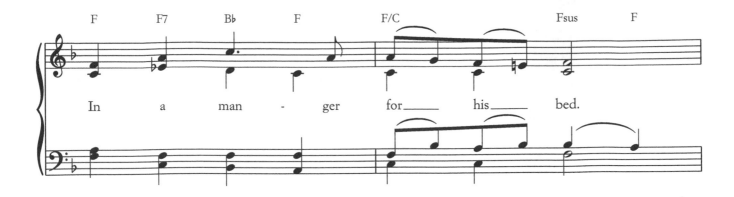

In a man - ger for___ his___ bed.

Ma - ry was that mo - ther mild,

Je - sus Christ her lit - tle___ child.

57

Once In Royal David's City

2
He came down to earth from heaven,
Who is God and Lord of all,
And his shelter was a stable,
And his cradle was a stall;
With the poor and mean and lowly,
Lived on earth our Saviour holy.

3
And through all his wond'rous childhood
He would honour and obey,
Love and watch the lowly maiden,
In whose gentle arms he lay;
Christian children all must be
Mild, obedient, good as He.

4
For He is our childhood's pattern,
Day by day like us he grew,
He was little, weak and helpless,
Tears and smiles like us he knew;
And he feeleth for our sadness,
And he shareth in our gladness.

5
And our eyes at last shall see him
Through his own redeeming love,
For that child so dear and gentle
Is our Lord in heaven above;
And he leads his children on
To the place where he is gone.

6
Not in that poor lowly stable,
With the oxen standing by,
We shall see him; but in heaven,
Set at God's right hand on high;
Where like stars his children crowned
All in white shall wait around.

See *Amid* The *Winter's* Snow

Words by **Edward Caswall**   *Music by John Goss*

Gently, not fast

See a-mid the win-ter's snow, Born for us on earth be-low; See the ten-der Lamb ap-pears, Prom-ised from e-ter-nal years. *Hail! thou ev-er*

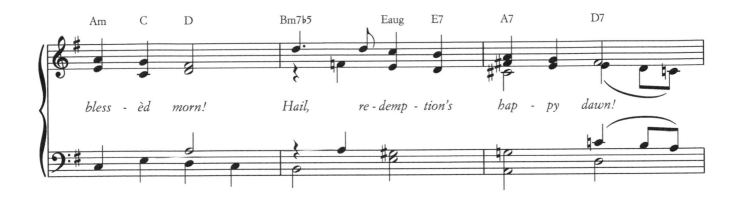

bless - èd morn! Hail, re - demp - tion's hap - py dawn!

Sing through all Je - ru - sa -lem, Christ is born in Beth - le - hem.

Chorus

Hail! thou ever blessed morn!
Hail, redemption's happy dawn!
Sing through all Jerusalem,
Christ is born in Bethlehem.

2
Lo, within a manger lies
He who built the starry skies;
He who, throned in heights sublime,
Sits amid the cherubim.
Hail, thou ever blessed morn…

3
Say, ye holy shepherds, say,
What your joyful news today?
Wherefore have ye left your sheep
On the lonely mountain steep?
Hail, thou ever blessed morn…

4
'As we watched at dead of night,
Lo, we saw a wond'rous light;
Angels, singing peace on earth,
Told us of the Saviour's birth.'
Hail, thou ever blessed morn…

5
Sacred infant, all divine,
What a tender love was thine,
Thus to come from highest bliss,
Down to such a world as this!
Hail, thou ever blessed morn…

6
Virgin mother, Mary blest,
By the joys that fill thy breast,
Pray for us, that we may prove
Worthy of the Saviour's love.
Hail, thou ever blessed morn…

Silent Night

Words by **Joseph Mohr**   *Music by* **Franz Gruber**

Ho - ly in - fant so ten - der and mild,

Sleep in heav - en - ly peace,_____

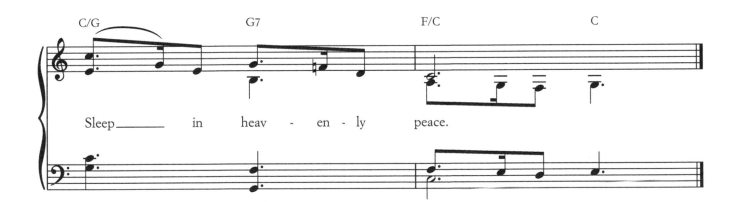

Sleep_____ in heav - en - ly peace.

2 Silent night, holy night.
Shepherds quake at the sight,
Glories stream from heaven afar,
Heav'nly hosts sing alleluia:
Christ, the Saviour is born,
Christ, the Saviour is born.

3 Silent night, holy night.
Son of God, love's pure light,
Radiant beams from thy holy face,
With the dawn of redeeming grace:
Jesus, Lord, at thy birth,
Jesus, Lord, at thy birth.

Sussex *Carol*

Traditional

Brightly

On Christ - mas night all Christ - ians sing, to hear the

news___ the an - gels bring. On Christ - mas night all

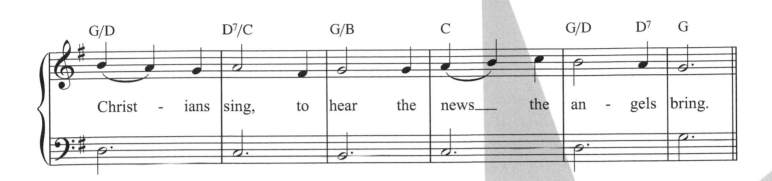

Christ - ians sing, to hear the news___ the an - gels bring.

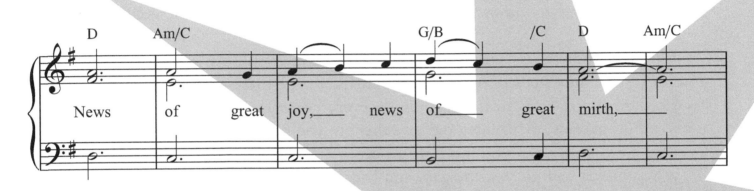

News of great joy,___ news of___ great mirth,___

63

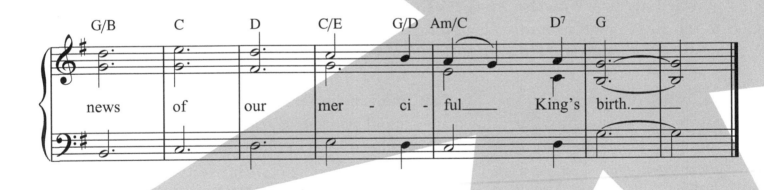

news of our mer - ci - ful___ King's birth.___

Then why should men on earth be so sad,
Since our redeemer made us glad.
2 Then why should men on earth be so sad,
Since our redeemer made us glad.
When from our sin he set us free,
All for to gain our liberty?

All out of darkness we have light,
Which made the angels sing this night:
3 All out of darkness we have light,
Which made the angels sing this night:
"Glory to God and peace to men,
Now and forever more, Amen."

The *Castle* Of *Ice* from *The* Snow *Queen* by *Hans* Christian *Andersen*

They stopped at a small house. It was a miserable place, whose roof came almost down to the ground, and whose door was so low that the family had to crawl on their stomachs whenever they wanted to go in or out. Except for an old Lapp woman, who was cooking fish over an oil stove, there was nobody in the house. The reindeer told her Gerda's story, but first of all he told his own, which seemed to him to be much more important. And Gerda was so pinched with the cold that she couldn't speak.

'Oh! you poor dears!' said the Lapp woman. 'You've still got a long way to go. You must travel hundreds of miles into Finnmark, for it's there that the Snow Queen lives in the country and burns Bengal lights every evening. I'll write a few words on a dry cod – I haven't any paper – and give them to you for the Finn woman who lives up there. She can tell can you more than I can.'

When Gerda had got warm again and had had something to eat and drink, the Lapp woman wrote a few words on a dried cod, told Gerda to take great care of it, and tied her firmly on the reindeer's back again, and off they went. Whizz! bang! up in the air the most beautiful blue Northern Lights glowed all night long. At last they reached Finnmark and knocked at the Finn woman's chimney, for she hadn't even got a door!

Inside it was so hot that the Finn woman herself went about almost naked. She was small and dirty. She immediately undid little Gerda's clothes and pulled off her mittens and her shoes, otherwise she'd have been too hot. Then she put a piece of ice on the reindeer's head and read what was written on the cod. She read it three times, and then she knew it by heart, so she popped the fish into the cooking pot, for it might just as well be eaten, and she never wasted anything.

Then the reindeer told first his own story and then little Gerda's. The Finn woman blinked her wise eyes, but said nothing.

'You are very wise,' said the reindeer. 'I know that you can bind all the winds together with one piece of cotton. When the pilot undoes the first knot, he gets a fair wind; when he undoes the second, it begins to blow hard; and when he undoes the third and the fourth knots, then comes a tempest that blows down the forests! Won't you prepare a potion for the little girl that will give her the strength of twelve men, and so let her overcome the Snow Queen?'

'The strength of twelve men?' said the Finn woman. 'That would be worth having, certainly.'

She went over to a shelf and took from it a large rolled-up pelt and opened it. On it strange letters were written, and the Finn woman read it until the perspiration poured down from her forehead.

But the reindeer begged so hard on little Gerda's behalf, and Gerda looked at the Finn woman with such beseeching eyes, full of tears, that she began once more to blink her own eyes; then she drew the reindeer into a corner, where they whispered together, and she put some more ice on his head.

'Little Kay is with the Snow Queen sure enough and he is finding everything there very much to his liking, and thinks it the best place in the world. But that's because he has a splinter of glass in his heart and a grain of glass in his eye. They must be got out first of all; otherwise he'll never become a human being again, and the Snow Queen will retain her power over him.'

'But can't you give Gerda something that will give her power over everything?'

'I can give her no greater power than that which she now possesses. Don't you see how great it is? Don't you see how men and beasts are compelled to serve her, and how wonderfully she has covered the wide world on her bare feet? She cannot get her power from us; it's there, in her heart, just because she is a sweet and innocent child. If she can't herself make her way to the Snow Queen and get the bits of glass out of Kay, then we cannot help her. Two miles from here the Snow Queen's garden begins. You can carry the little girl as far as that, and put her down beside a bush with red berries standing in the snow. Don't stop and chatter, but hurry straight back here.' The Finn woman then lifted Gerda on to the reindeer, who ran off as fast as he could.

'Oh! I haven't got my boots! I haven't got my mittens!' cried little Gerda. In the bitter cold she noticed it at once. But the reindeer dared not stop; he ran on until they reached the bush with the red berries. There he set Gerda down and kissed

her on the mouth. Great big tears rolled down the animal's cheeks, and then he ran back as fast as he could go. And there stood poor Gerda, without shoes and without gloves in the middle of the terrible, ice-cold Finnmark.

She ran forward as fast as she could. Towards her came a whole regiment of snowflakes; but they were not falling from the sky, which was quite clear and bright with the Northern Lights. The snowflakes ran along the ground, and the nearer they came, the bigger they grew. Gerda remembered how big and wonderfully made the snowflakes had looked that time when she had seen them through the magnifying glass. But these here were certainly much bigger and much more frightening. They were alive; they were the Snow Queen's guards, and they had strange shapes. Some of them looked like great ugly hedgehogs; others like a bunches of knotted snakes, sticking their heads out; and others again were like small, fat bears, whose hair stood on end. All were dazzling white, and all were living snowflakes.

Little Gerda said the Lord's prayer. And the cold was so great that she could see her own breath coming out of her mouth like smoke. It grew thicker and thicker and formed itself into little Angels, who grew bigger and bigger as soon as they reached the ground. All had helmets on their heads and spears and shields in their hands. Their numbers became greater and greater, and by the time Gerda had finished the Lord's prayer, there was a whole legion of them. They charged with their spears against the hateful snowflakes, so that they were splintered into a hundred pieces; and little Gerda went forward confidently and with a stout heart. The Angels stroked her hands and feet, and immediately she felt the cold less and hastened on to the Snow Queen's castle.

But now, before we go any further, we must see what Kay was doing. He certainly wasn't thinking about little Gerda, and least of all that she was standing there outside the castle.

The walls of the castle were built of the driven snow, and the windows and doors of the cutting wind. There were more than a hundred halls, all just as the snow had formed them. The biggest of them was many miles long, and the strong north light illumined them all, however vast and empty, and however cold and glittering they were. Here there was never any fun, not even a dancing bear, though the storm might have played for it and polar bears might have stood on their hind legs and done their pretty tricks; never a little party to play Slap-mouth or Pat-paw; never even a coffee party for the white lady foxes. Empty, big and cold were the halls of the Snow Queen's

castle. The Northern Lights shone so steadily that you could tell exactly when they were at their highest and when at their lowest. In the midst of these unending empty halls of snow was a frozen lake, broken into a thousand pieces. But each piece was exactly like the others, and the whole was a perfect work of art. And in the middle of the lake sat the Snow Queen, when she was home, and then she used to say that she sat in the in Mirror of Wisdom and that it was the only one, and the best in the world.

Little Kay was blue with cold indeed, almost black; but he didn't notice it, for she had kissed away the shudders of cold from him, and his heart was like a lump of ice. He was pushing a number of sharp-edged, flat pieces of ice about, pushing and pulling them this way and that, as if he were trying to make something, just as you may have a lot of little pieces of wood and try to make patterns with them in what is called a Chinese Puzzle. Kay went on making patterns, and some of them were truly wonderful. That was the Intellectual Ice Game. In his eyes the patterns were absolutely marvellous and of the greatest importance. That was because of the grain of glass in his eye. He made perfect patterns which formed written words; but he never succeeded in laying the bits to make the word he wanted, the word Eternity. The Snow Queen had said: 'If you can find out that pattern, then you shall be your own master, and I will give you the whole world and a new pair of skates.' But he couldn't do it.

'Now I shall fly away to the warm lands,' said the Snow Queen. 'I will go there and look into the black pots!' (That was what they called the fire-spitting mountains, Etna and Vesuvius). 'I'll make them a little white! That's as it should be! It's good for the lemons and vines.' And the Snow Queen flew away, and Kay sat all alone in the great empty Ice Halls, mile upon mile of them, and gazed at the ice fragments and thought and thought until he crackled. Stiff and quiet he sat there; you'd have thought he was frozen.

Just at that moment little Gerda stepped through the great gate into the castle. A cutting wind was howling, but she said an evening prayer and the winds died down as if they meant to go to sleep; and she stepped into the big empty cold halls. Then she saw Kay, recognised him, and flew to him and put her arms round his neck. She held him fast and cried: 'Kay! darling little Kay! At last I have found you!'

But he sat quite still and stiff and cold. Then little Gerda wept hot tears, which fell on to his breast. They sank into his heart and melted the lump of ice that was there and destroyed the splinter of glass.

Kay looked at her and she sang:

'Where roses grow in the hedgerows wild,
There we meet the Holy Child'.

Then Kay started to weep. He wept so hard that the grain of glass swam out of his eye, and then he recognised her and cried joyfully: 'Gerda! Darling little Gerda! Where have you been for so long? And where have I been?' And he looked round. 'How cold it is here! How big and empty!'' And he held fast to Gerda, and she laughed and cried for joy. It was all so wonderful that the very ice chips danced round for joy, and when they got tired and sat down, they arranged themselves exactly so as to make those letters, which the Snow Queen had said that if he could find, then he would be his own master, and she would give him the whole world and a new pair of skates.

Gerda kissed his cheeks and they began to glow; she kissed his eyes, and they shone like her own; she kissed his hands and feet, and he became healthy and full of spirit. The Snow Queen could come home now! His release stood there, written in letters of glittering ice!

They took each other by the hand and wandered out of the great castle. They talked about their grandmother and the roses on the roof. And wherever they went, the wind was stilled and the sun shone. When they came to the bush with the red berries, there stood the reindeer waiting for them. He had brought another young reindeer with him; her udders were full, and she gave the children warm milk and kissed them on the mouth.

Then they carried Kay and Gerda first to the Finn woman, where they got nice and warm in the hot room and were told exactly how to get home, and then to the Lapp woman, who had made new clothes for them and put their sledge in good order.

The reindeer and the young doe ran along beside them and accompanied them to the boundary of the land, where the first green things were sprouting. There they took leave of the Lapp woman and the reindeers. 'Goodbye!' cried everybody. And the first little birds began to twitter and there were green buds in the woods, out of which, mounted on a magnificent horse (Gerda recognised it – it had been harnessed to the golden coach) there rode a young maiden with a splendid red cap on her head, and pistols in her holsters. It was the little robber maid, who was tired of staying at home and was now setting out towards the North, or later, if that didn't suit her, to some

other part of the world. She recognised Gerda at once, and Gerda recognised her, and there was great joy. 'You're a fine sort of a fellow to go careering all over the world after!' said the robber maid to little Kay. 'I wonder if you're worth it!'

But Gerda patted her cheeks and asked about the Prince and Princess.

'They have gone abroad,' said the robber maid.

'And the crow?' asked Gerda.

'Oh! the crow is dead,' she replied. 'The tame sweetheart has become a widow and goes about with a little piece of black cloth round her leg. She complains bitterly; but that's all my eye! But now tell how you got on and how you managed to get him away.'

And Gerda and Kay told her.

'Snip-snap-slipperty-slap!' said the robber maid, shook them both by the hand and promised that if she ever came to their town, she would come and see them. And then off she rode into the wide world.

Gerda and Kay went on hand in hand, and as they went along it was beautifully spring all round them, with flowers and green foliage. The church bells rang, and they recognised the high towers and the town – it was the very town in which they lived. They entered it and went straight to their grandmother's door, up the stairs and into the room, where everything was just as it had been before. The clock was going tick! tock! and the hands moved round. But as they went through the door they saw that they had become grown-up people. The roses on the roof turned their blossoms towards the open window, and there still stood the little children's stools. And Gerda and Kay went and sat down, each on their own and held hands. The cold, empty magnificence in the Snow Queen's castle they had forgotten like a bad dream. Their grandmother sat in God's sunshine and read aloud from the Bible: 'Except ye become as little children, ye shall in on wise enter the Kingdom of Heaven.' And Kay and Gerda gazed into each other's eyes, and suddenly they understood the meaning of the old hymn:

'Where roses grow in the hedgerows wild,
There we meet the Holy Child.'

There they both sat, grown-up yet still children, children in their hearts; and it was summer – warm, kindly summer.

The *First* Nowell

Traditional

Brightly

The_ first____ No - well the_ an - gel did say Was to

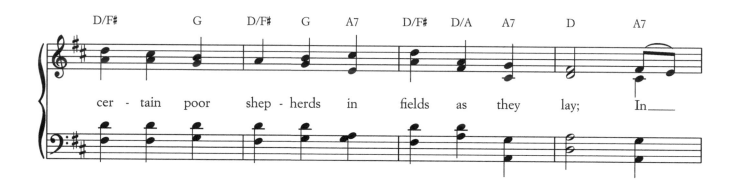

cer - tain poor shep - herds in fields as they lay; In____

fields____ where_ they lay____ keep - ing their sheep, On a

cold win - ter's night____ that was____ so deep: *No* -

well, _____ No - well, No - well, No - well,

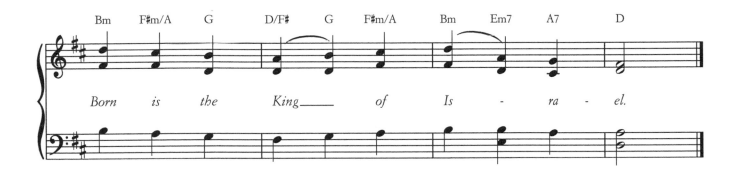

Born is the King _____ of Is - ra - el.

Chorus *Nowell, Nowell, Nowell, Nowell,*
Born is the King of Israel.

2 They lookèd up and saw a star,
Shining in the east, beyond them far,
And to the earth it gave great light,
And so it continued both day and night.
Nowell, Nowell…

3 And by the light of that same star,
Three wise men came from country far;
To seek for a king was their intent,
And to follow the star where'er it went.
Nowell, Nowell…

4 This star drew nigh to the north-west,
O'er Bethlehem it took its rest,
And there it did both stop and stay
Right over the place where Jesus lay.
Nowell, Nowell…

5 Then entered in those wise men three,
Full rev'rently upon their knee,
And offered there in his presence,
Their gold and myrrh and frankincense.
Nowell, Nowell…

6 Then let us all with one accord
Sing praises to our heav'nly Lord,
That hath made heav'n and earth of naught,
And with his blood mankind hath bought.
Nowell, Nowell…

TRACK 24

The *Holly* And *The* Ivy

Traditional

At a moderate pace

The hol-ly and the i-vy, When they are both full-grown, Of__ all the trees that are in the wood, The__ hol-ly bears the crown. *O the ris-ing of the*

sun,___ And the run-ning of the deer, The___ play-ing of the

mer - ry or - gan, Sweet sing - ing in the choir.

Chorus

O the rising of the sun,
And the running of the deer,
The playing of the merry organ,
Sweet singing in the choir.

2
The holly bears a blossom,
White as the lily flow'r,
And Mary bore sweet Jesus Christ
To be our sweet Saviour.
O the rising…

3
The holly bears a berry,
As red as any blood,
And Mary bore sweet Jesus Christ
To do poor sinners good.
O the rising…

4
The holly bears a prickle,
As sharp as any thorn,
And Mary bore sweet Jesus Christ
On Christmas Day in the morn.
O the rising…

5
The holly bears a bark,
As bitter as any gall,
And Mary bore sweet Jesus Christ
For to redeem us all.
O the rising…

The *Twelve* Days Of Christmas

Traditional

Lively

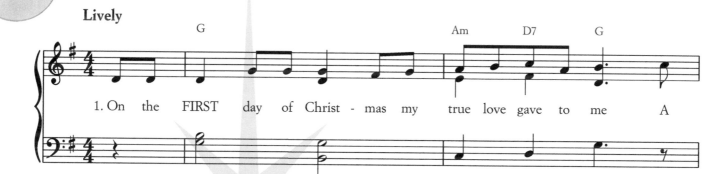

1. On the FIRST day of Christ - mas my true love gave to me A

par - tridge in a pear tree. 2. On the SEC-OND day of Christ - mas my

true love gave to me Two tur - tle doves, and a par - tridge in a pear

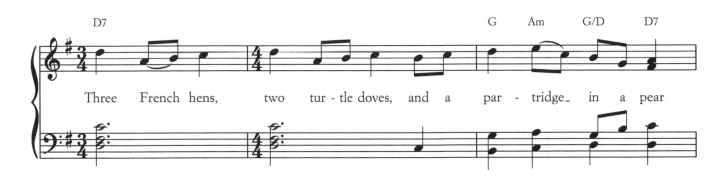

FIFTH day of Christ - mas my true love gave to me Five gold

rings, four_ call - ing birds, three French hens,

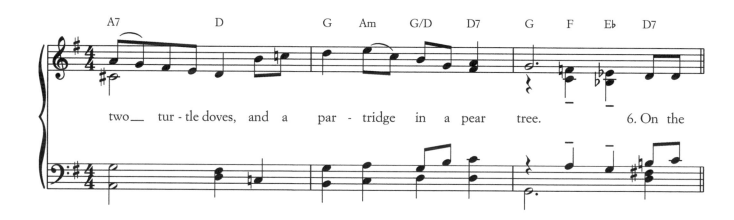

two_ tur - tle doves, and a par - tridge in a pear tree. 6. On the

SIXTH
SEVENTH
EIGHTH
NINTH day of Christ - mas my true love gave to me
TENTH
ELEVENTH
TWELFTH

Repeat this bar in reverse order as necessary

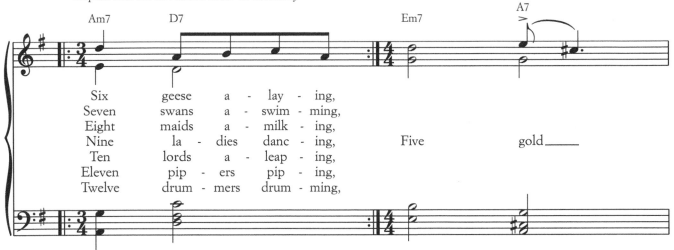

Six geese a - lay - ing,
Seven swans a - swim - ming,
Eight maids a - milk - ing,
Nine la - dies danc - ing,   Five gold___
Ten lords a - leap - ing,
Eleven pip - ers pip - ing,
Twelve drum - mers drum - ming,

rings, four___ call - ing birds, three French hens,

two___ tur - tle doves, and a par - tridge in a pear tree.   7. On the

par - tridge___ in a pear tree.

On the SECOND day of Christmas my true love gave to me
Two turtle doves, and a partridge in a pear tree.

On the THIRD day of Christmas my true love gave to me
Three French hens, two turtle doves,
and a partridge in a pear tree.

On the FOURTH day of Christmas my true love gave to me
Four calling birds...

On the FIFTH day of Christmas my true love gave to me
Five gold rings...

On the SIXTH day of Christmas my true love gave to me
Six geese a-laying...

On the SEVENTH day of Christmas my true love gave to me
Seven swans a-swimming...

On the EIGHTH day of Christmas my true love gave to me
Eight maids a-milking...

On the NINTH day of Christmas my true love gave to me
Nine ladies dancing...

On the TENTH day of Christmas my true love gave to me
Ten lords a-leaping...

On the ELEVENTH day of Christmas my true love gave to me
Eleven pipers piping...

On the TWELTH day of Christmas my true love gave to me
Twelve drummers drumming, eleven pipers piping,
ten lords a-leaping, nine ladies dancing,
eight maids a-milking, seven swans a-swimming,
six geese a-laying, five gold rings, four calling birds,
three French hens, two turtle doves,
and a partridge in a pear tree.

When Santa Claus Comes
Anon

A good time is coming, I wish it were here,
The very best time in the whole of the year;
I'm counting each day on my fingers and thumbs,
The weeks that must pass before Santa Claus comes.

Then when the first snowflakes begin to come down,
And the wind whistles sharp and the branches are brown,
I'll not mind the cold, though my fingers it numbs,
For it brings the time nearer when Santa Claus comes.

The *Box* Of *Magic*
by *Malorie* Blackman

It was Christmas Eve, but Peter was in no hurry. His head bent, Peter dragged his feet as he made his way slowly home. There was no point in rushing. Mum and Dad would only be arguing about something or another. Peter and his sister Chloe had hoped that the quarrelling would stop over Christmas. It hadn't. If anything, it'd got worse.

Peter had spent all afternoon searching and searching for the perfect present for his Mum and Dad. Something that would stop them quarrelling for just five minutes. Something that would make Christmas the way it used to be, with smiles and songs and happiness in every corner of the house. But all the searching had been for nothing. Peter didn't have that much money to begin with and all the things he could afford, he didn't want. All the gifts he could afford looked so cheap and tacky that Peter knew they would fall apart about ten seconds after they were handled. What was he going to do? He had to buy something and time was running out.

Then he caught sight of it out of the corner of his eye. The medium-sized sign above the door said 'THE CHRISTMAS SHOP' in spidery writing. The small shop window was framed with silver and gold tinsel and a scattering of glitter like mini stars. At the bottom of the window, fake snow had been sprayed. It looked so much like the real thing that had it been outside the window instead of inside, Peter would've been sure it was real snow. A single Christmas tree, laden down with fairy lights and baubles and yet more tinsel, stood proudly in the exact centre of the window.

Peter stood in front of the shop and stared. He'd never seen anything so… wonderful! It was as if Christmas had started in this shop and then spread out to cover the whole wide world.

"The Christmas Shop…" Peter muttered to himself.

He wondered why he'd never seen it before. True, it was behind the shopping precinct

and he usually walked through the precinct not around it, but even so. Peter looked up and down the street. The few other shops in the same row as The Christmas Shop were all boarded up.

Unexpectedly, the shop door opened. A tall portly man with a white beard and a merry twinkle in his eyes stood in the doorway.

"Hello! Come in! Come in!" the shopkeeper beckoned.

"I... er... don't have much money."

Peter shook his head.

"No matter. Come in."

The shopkeeper turned and held the door open. It was as if there was no doubt in his mind that Peter would enter. Uncertainly, Peter dithered on the pavement. He hadn't intended to go in. He was only window shopping. But the shop looked so warm and inviting and the shopkeeper seemed so friendly. Peter walked into the shop. And he gasped in amazement!

It was even better inside than it had appeared from outside. It smelt of freshly baked bread and warm cakes and toast and cinnamon and nutmeg and it was so warm; it was as if the sun itself had come for a visit.

"Isn't my shop the best!" smiled the shopkeeper. "Look around. Feel free. You can pick up anything, touch anything."

Peter stared at the shopkeeper. He certainly wasn't like any other shopkeeper Peter had ever met. Usually shopkeepers didn't like school kids in their shops and they certainly didn't like them touching things. Peter wandered around the shop, his dark brown eyes wide with delight. Toys and games and Christmas sweets and Christmas treats filled every corner.

Peter's hand curled around the money in his pocket. He could buy all his Christmas presents in here. Peter bent his head to examine a gold and berry-red scarf. That would be perfect for his mum. And maybe the night-blue and yellow scarf for his dad. And he could get that little glass unicorn over there for Chloe. That was just the kind of thing she liked. The strange thing was, none of the items had prices on them.

"H-How much are these woolly scarves?" Peter asked, crossing his fingers in his pockets. "And how much is that unicorn over there?"

"That depends on who they're for and why you think they'd like them," answered the shopkeeper.

"The scarves are for my Mum and Dad and the unicorn is for my sister. Chloe likes things made of glass. She keeps them in her bedroom on the window-sill. And I thought that Mum and Dad could have the scarves to keep them warm."

"And how much money do you have?" asked the shopkeeper.

Peter took out all the money in his pocket. The shopkeeper checked through it carefully.

"You're lucky," said the shopkeeper. "You've got enough for all the things you want."

"I have? Really?" Peter couldn't believe it.

The shopkeeper smiled and nodded. Peter grinned at him, but slowly his smile faded. He'd buy the scarves for his Mum and Dad and then what? What good would any present do? Peter could see it now. Mum and Dad opening their presents on Christmas Day.

"Thanks Peter. That's great," says Dad.

"Peter, that's wonderful," says Mum.

And then they'd fling their presents to the back of the chair and start shouting at each other again.

"What's the matter, Peter?" asked the shopkeeper gently.

Peter jumped. He'd been lost in a world of his own.

"It's just that... Hang on a second. How did you know my name?" Peter stared.

"It's a little game of mine," the shopkeeper beamed. "I like to guess people's names, and nine times out of ten, I get it right."

Peter was impressed.

"So you were saying?" the shopkeeper prompted.

"I ... I don't suppose you've got anything in your shop to stop my Mum and Dad from fighting?"

The moment the words were out of his mouth, Peter regretted it. What was he doing? He hadn't told anyone about his Mum and Dad, not even his best friend Andy. No one knew how things were at home except his sister Chloe, and she didn't talk about it either.

"Oh, I see. Do your Mum and Dad argue a lot?" asked the shopkeeper.

"All the time," Peter sighed.

The shopkeeper pursed his lips.

"Hhmm! I think I have just the present you need – for your whole family."

The shopkeeper went around his brightly coloured counter and disappeared down behind it. Moments later he straightened up, a huge smile on his face and a silver box in his hands.

"These are what you need," he said.

"What are they?" Peter asked doubtfully.

"Christmas crackers," announced the shopkeeper proudly. At the disappointed look on Peter's face, he added, "Ah, but they're not just any crackers. They're magic. Guaranteed to work, or your money back."

"How are they magic?" Peter asked suspiciously.

"The magic only works if they're pulled on Christmas Day, when you're all around the table eating dinner," explained the shopkeeper.

"But how do they work?"

"It's hard to explain. You have to see the magic for yourself."

"How much are they?" asked Peter, still doubtful. Maybe he could buy them and still get the other presents as well.

"I'm afraid they're very expensive because they're magic," said the shopkeeper. "They'll cost you all the money you've got, and even then I'm letting you have them cheap."

Peter thought for a moment. Magic crackers. Crackers that would actually stop Mum and Dad from arguing. They were worth the money if they could do that. He took a deep breath.

"All right, I'll take them," he said quickly, before he could change his mind.

Peter handed over his money and the shopkeeper handed over the box of eight crackers. Moments later, Peter was out of the shop and running all the way home. Magic crackers! He couldn't wait for Christmas Day.

"I've been in that kitchen since seven o'clock this morning. I think the least you could do is sit at the table with the rest of your family." Mum's voice dripped with ice.

"I want to watch the end of this film," Dad argued.

"Typical! You're so selfish," Mum snapped.

Peter and Chloe looked at each other and sighed. Mum and Dad were at it again. Christmas Day – and they were still arguing.

"Dad, you and Mum and Chloe can open my present now," Peter said desperately. "The man in The Christmas Shop said they should only be opened when we're all sitting round the table eating dinner."

"Oh, all right then," Dad grumbled.

"Oh, I see. You'll come to the table if Peter asks you to, but not if I ask you," sniffed Mum.

"Peter doesn't nag me every two seconds," Dad said as he sat down at the table.

Chloe shook her head and turned to look out of the window. Peter ran to get the present he'd bought. It was the only one left unopened under the tree. He stood between his Mum and Dad, putting the present down on the tablecloth. Mum and Dad looked at each other.

"Go on then," Dad prompted.

"You do it," said Mum.

"I'll do it," said Chloe. She tore off the bright red and yellow wrapping paper. "It's a box of crackers," she said, surprised.

"Not just any crackers," Peter said eagerly. "They're magic crackers!"

"Who told you that?" Mum smiled.

"The man in The Christmas Shop," Peter replied.

"Well, let's all sit down. Then we can pull them and get on with our dinner," said Dad, adding under his breath, "And maybe then I can get back to my film."

But the moment they all sat down, something peculiar began to happen. A strange feeling settled over the dinner table. A hopeful, expectant feeling – as if, in spite of themselves, everyone was waiting for something terrific, amazing and spectacular to happen all at once. The noise from the telly was just a distant hum at the other end of the room. Light, like warm spring sunshine, came from everyone, smiling at everyone else as they watched Dad place two crackers beside each plate. Chloe held out her cracker to Dad. Peter held his Christmas cracker out to Mum.

"One! Two! Three!" they all shouted.

Bang! Pop! The sound of exploding crackers filled the room. Chloe and Peter got the biggest parts of the crackers. They both peered down into them.

"They're... they're empty!" Chloe exclaimed.

"No! They can't be," frowned Mum.

"See for yourself," said Chloe, handing over her cracker.

Peter couldn't believe it. Empty... When he remembered the smiling, friendly face

of the jolly man with the white beard in The Christmas Shop, he just couldn't believe it. That man wouldn't take his money and sell him a box of nothing – Peter was sure he wouldn't. And yet... and yet, his cracker was empty. Just an empty roll covered with some glossy paper and nothing else. No hats. No jokes. No gifts. Nothing.

"Maybe there were just two duff ones in the box," Mum suggested.

Mum and Dad pulled their crackers next. The same thing happened. They were empty. Chloe and Peter pulled crackers five and six at the same time as Mum and Dad pulled crackers seven and eight.

They were all empty.

Peter examined each one, hoping against hope that they'd got it wrong or it was a trick – but it wasn't. Peter looked at Chloe, then Mum and Dad – and burst into tears. He couldn't help it.

"The shopkeeper told me they were magic crackers," Peter sobbed to Mum and Dad. "I only bought them because he said they would make you stop arguing with each other. He promised me they were magic. He *promised* me..."

Dad stared. Mum's mouth fell open.

"You...you bought them – because of us?" Dad asked, aghast.

Peter sniffed and nodded.

"Never mind, Peter." Chloe put her arm around her younger brother's shoulder. "Besides, nothing would stop Mum and Dad from fighting. Not even a real box of magic crackers."

And with that, Chloe burst into tears too.

"Chloe! Peter!" Mum and Dad ran around the table to hug Peter and Chloe to them. "We had no idea we were quarrelling that much."

"And we had no idea we were upsetting both of you so much," said Dad.

But Peter and Chloe couldn't stop crying.

"I'll tell you what," said Mum. "Let's make our own Christmas crackers. All this food will stay warm in the oven until we've finished."

"Terrific idea."

Dad went over to the telly and switched it off.

"We'll make the hats first," Dad continued, "Out of newspaper."

Dad and Mum showed Peter and Chloe how to make sailor hats out of newspaper. That took about five minutes. Then they all sat down for dinner. Over dinner, everyone had to tell the worst jokes they knew, like, 'How do you make an

apple puff? Chase it round the garden!' and 'Why did the elephant cross the road? Because it was the chicken's day off!'

Dad's joke was 'Why did silly Billy stand on a ladder when he was learning to sing? So he could reach the high notes!' And Mum's joke was ancient but she was still proud of it! 'How do you make a Swiss Roll? Push him down a hill!' Chloe told a joke that Peter didn't get until Mum explained it. 'How do you tell how old a telephone is? Count its rings!' (Mum explained that you could tell the age of a tree by counting the rings through its trunk.) Everyone got Peter's joke. 'Why are vampires crazy? Because they're often bats!' And when anyone ran out of jokes, they made them up, which was even funnier!

After dinner when everyone was eating Christmas pudding, Mum grabbed Dad and whispered in his ear. Suddenly they both dashed off upstairs with the empty crackers. Ten minutes later they reappeared with the various ends of each cracker now glued together.

"Cracker time!" said Mum. And she held out a cracker to Chloe.

They both pulled.

"POP!" shouted Mum.

Chloe looked inside the cracker and there was one of Mum's old bangles – the gold and blue one which had always been Chloe's favourite.

"Your turn," said Dad, holding out a cracker to Peter. They both shouted, "BANG!"

Peter looked inside the cracker. There was a pig made of Lego bricks. At least, that's what Peter thought it was.

"It's not a pig. It's a rocket!" said Dad indignantly.

Mum started to giggle.

"I told you it looked more like a pig, dear," she said.

They 'popped' the rest of the crackers. They all had very silly, very tacky, very wonderful presents in them.

"Who needs rotten, mouldy old crackers?" asked Dad. "We can do it all ourselves."

"And they're much better too," Mum agreed. "It's just a shame that Peter got conned out of his money. Where did you say the shop was?"

"Behind the precinct. All the other shops on the same street were boarded up," Peter replied.

"There aren't any shops behind the precinct. The last one closed down over a year ago," Dad frowned.

"There's one still open. It's called The Christmas Shop," said Peter.

Mum and Dad looked at each other. They both shrugged.

"Never mind. I'd say they were the best crackers we've ever had," smiled Mum. "My jaw still aches from laughing at all those terrible jokes."

"Those crackers were... a box of magic," said Dad, giving Mum a cuddle.

Later that night, as Peter lay in bed, he still couldn't quite believe what had happened. Mum and Dad hadn't argued once since the crackers had been pulled. In fact, it was the most wonderful day they'd all had in a long, long time. The only cloud was the shopkeeper who'd sold Peter the crackers in the first place. Peter still didn't want to believe that the shopkeeper was a crook who had deliberately diddled him out of his money.

Suddenly, a strange tinkling-clinking came from across the room, followed by a plopping sound. Peter sat up and frowned. What was that? He switched on his bedside light. There it was again – the same strange noise. And it seemed to be coming from his chair over by the window. Over the back of the chair were the jumper and the pair of trousers Peter had worn on Christmas Eve. That strange noise couldn't be coming from them – could it? Swallowing hard, Peter got up and tiptoed across to the chair.

Tinkle! Clinkle! Plop!

There it was again! Peter took a deep breath, counted to three, then quickly pulled the chair to one side. More money fell out of his trouser pockets and plopped on to the carpet. Peter's eyes goggled! Where had all that money come from? He scooped up the money on the floor, then picked up his trousers and dug into his pockets. There was more money inside them. He counted it all very carefully. It was the exact amount of money he had paid for the Christmas crackers...

Peter sat down on his bed and stared down at the money in his hand. What was going on? He shook his head and looked around the room hoping for some clue. Had Mum and Dad done it? Had they put the money in his pockets to make up for him losing his money in The Christmas Shop? But they didn't know exactly how

much he'd paid for the crackers. And now here he was, with the exact same coins in his hand.

Then something else caught his eye. There on his bed-side table, were all the Christmas cards he'd received from his friends. At the front was the card he'd got from his best friend Andy. Peter gasped and stared so hard, his eyes began to ache. The face on the card... Peter had seen that face before – in The Christmas Shop.

The shopkeeper and Father Christmas were one and the same person... Peter picked up the card and studied it. The shopkeeper *was* Father Christmas. Peter was sure of it. And that would explain how he'd got his money back. Which meant only one thing... The Christmas crackers *were* magic after all.

"Thank you," Peter whispered to the Christmas card. And he was sure that on the card, the smiling face of Father Christmas winked at him.

December
John Clare (1793-1864)

While snows the window-panes bedim,
*   The fire curls up a sunny charm,*
Where, creaming o'er the pitcher's rim,
*   The flowering ale is set to warm;*
Mirth, full of joy as summer bees,
*   Sits there, its pleasures to impart,*
And children, 'tween their parents' knees,
*   Sing scraps of carols o'er by heart.*

And some, to view the winter weathers,
*   Climb up the window-seat with glee,*
Likening the snow to falling feathers,
*   In fancy's infant ecstasy;*
Laughing, with superstitious love,
*   O'er visions wild that youth supplies,*
Of people pulling geese above,
*   And keeping Christmas in the skies.*

As tho' the homestead trees were drest,
*   In lieu of snow, with dancing leaves,*
As tho' the sun-dried martin's nest,
*   Instead of ickles, hung the eaves,*
The children hail the happy day –
*   As if the snow were April's grass,*
And pleas'd, as 'neath the warmth of May,
*   Sport o'er the water froze to glass.*

Unto Us A Boy Is Born

Traditional   *English Words by* **George Woodward**

Not fast

Un - to us a boy is born, King of all cre - a - tion,

Came he to a world for - lorn, The Lord of e - very na -

3 Herod then with fear was filled:
'A prince', he said 'in Jewry!'
All the little boys he killed
At Bethlem in his fury.

4 Now may Mary's Son who came
So long ago to love us,
Lead us all with hearts aflame
Unto the joys above us.

5 Omega and Alpha he!
Let the organ thunder,
While the choir with peals of glee,
Doth rend the air asunder.

We Three Kings Of Orient Are

Words & Music by **John Henry Hopkins**

Smooth and flowing

We three Kings of O - ri - ent are; Bear - ing gifts we tra-verse a - far,

Field and foun - tain, moor and moun - tain, Fol - low - ing yon - der

star: O_____ star of won - der, star of night,

Star with roy - al beau - ty bright, West - ward lead - ing,

still pro - ceed - ing, Guide us to thy per - fect light.

Chorus

O star of wonder, star of night,
Star with royal beauty bright,
Westward leading, still proceeding,
Guide us to thy perfect light.

2 Born a King on Bethlehem plain,
Gold I bring, to crown him again,
King for ever, ceasing never,
Over us all to reign.
O star of wonder, star of night...

3 Frankincense to offer have I,
Incense owns a Deity nigh,
Prayer and praising, gladly raising,
Worship him, God most high.
O star of wonder, star of night...

4 Myrrh is mine, its bitter perfume
Breathes a life of gathering gloom;
Sorrowing, sighing, bleeding, dying,
Sealed in the stone-cold tomb.
O star of wonder, star of night...

5 Glorious now behold him arise,
King and God and sacrifice;
Heaven sings alleluia,
Alleluia the earth replies.
O star of wonder, star of night...

We *Wish* You *A* Merry *Christmas*

Traditional

Brightly

| G | C | A | D |

We wish you a mer-ry Christ-mas, We wish you a mer-ry Christ-mas, We

| B | Em G | C Am D7 G |

wish you a mer-ry Christ-mas And a hap-py New Year. *Good*

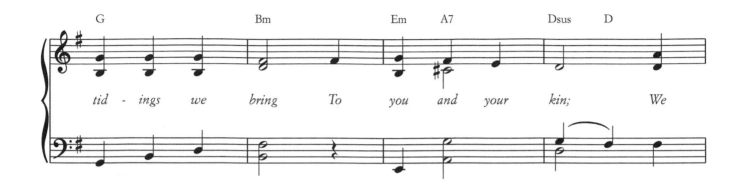

tid - ings we bring To you and your kin; We

wish you a mer - ry Christ - mas And a hap - py New Year.

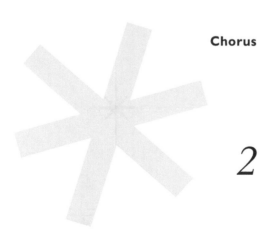

Chorus

Good tidings we bring
To you and your kin;
We wish you a merry Christmas
And a happy New Year.

2

We all want some figgy pudding,
We all want some figgy pudding,
We all want some figgy pudding,
So bring some out here!
Good tidings we bring...

3

We won't go until we get some,
We won't go until we get some,
We won't go until we get some,
So bring some out here!
Good tidings we bring...

While *Shepherds* Watched

Music **Traditional**   Words by **Nahum Tate**

Moderately

While   shep - herds watched   their   flocks   by   night,   All

seat - ed on the ground, The an - gel of the

Lord came down, And glo - ry shone a - round.

2 'Fear not,' said he (for mighty dread
Had seized their troubled mind);
'Glad tidings of great joy I bring
To you and all mankind.'

3 'To you in David's town this day
Is born of David's line
A Saviour, who is Christ the Lord;
And this shall be the sign:'

4 'The heav'nly babe you there shall find
To human view displayed,
All meanly wrapped in swathing bands,
And in a manger laid.'

5 Thus spake the seraph, and forthwith
Appeared a shining throng
Of angels praising God, who thus
Addressed their joyful song:

6 'All glory be to God on high,
And to the earth be peace;
Goodwill henceforth from heav'n to men
Begin and never cease.'

The Oxen
Thomas Hardy (1840-70)

Christmas Eve, and twelve of the clock,
'Now they are all on their knees,'
An elder said as we sat in a flock
By the embers in hearthside ease.

We pictured the meek mild creatures where
They dwelt in their strawy pen,
Nor did it occur to one of us there,
To doubt they were kneeling then.

So fair a fancy few would weave
In these years! Yet, I feel,
If someone said on Christmas Eve
'Come; see the oxen kneel

'In the lonely barton by yonder coomb
Our childhood used to know,'
I should go with him in the gloom,
Hoping it might be so.

A Christmas Carol
Christina Rossetti (1830-94)

In the bleak mid-winter
Frosty wind made moan,
Earth stood hard as iron,
Water like a stone;
Snow had fallen, snow on snow,
Snow on snow,
In the bleak mid-winter,
Long ago.

Our God, Heaven cannot hold Him
Nor earth sustain;
Heaven and earth shall flee away
When He comes to reign:
In the bleak mid-winter
A stable place sufficed
The Lord God Almighty
Jesus Christ.

Blow, Blow, Thou Winter Wind
William Shakespeare (1564-1616)
from 'As You Like It'

Blow, blow, thou winter wind,
Thou art not so unkind
As man's ingratitude;
Thy tooth is not so keen,
Because thou art not seen,
Although thy breath be rude.

Heigh-ho! sing, heigh-ho! unto the green holly:
Most friendship is feigning, most loving mere folly.
Then heigh-ho! the holly!
This life is most jolly.

Freeze, freeze, thou bitter sky,
That dost not bite so nigh
As benefits forgot:
Though thou the waters warp,
Thy sting is not so sharp
As friend remember'd not

Heigh-ho! sing, heigh-ho! unto the green holly:
Most friendship is feigning, most loving merely folly.
Then heigh-ho! the holly!
This life is most jolly.